TOUCHSTONES
VOLUME A
Texts for Discussion

Selected, translated, and edited
by
Geoffrey Comber
Howard Zeiderman
Nicholas Maistrellis

Published by
TOUCHSTONES
DISCUSSION PROJECT

About the Touchstones Discussion Project

The Touchstones Discussion Project is a nonprofit organization founded on the belief that all people can benefit from the listening, speaking, thinking, and interpersonal skills gained by engaging in active, focused discussions. Since 1984, Touchstones has helped millions of students and others develop and improve these skills in school, work, and life. For more information about the Touchstones Discussion Project, visit www.touchstones.org.

Touchstones Discussion Project
522 Chesapeake Avenue
Annapolis, Maryland 21403
800-456-6542
www.touchstones.org

ISBN: 1-878461-57-5

ACKNOWLEDGEMENTS

We would like to thank the following for their help in the publication of this volume:

The National Gallery of Art, Washington, DC, for permission to reproduce:
Portrait; Rembrandt Van Rijn; Widener Collection.
Self-Portrait; Rembrandt Van Rijn;
Andrew W. Mellon Collection.

The Baltimore Museum of Art; for permission to reproduce:
from The Cone Collection, formed by Dr. Claribel Cone and Miss Elta Cone of Baltimore, Maryland BMA 1950.196
Mont St. Victoire Seen From The Bibemus Quarry; Paul Cezanne.

The following works are also reprinted by permission:
"Buddy," by Langston Hughes. Reprinted by permission of Harold Ober Associates, Inc. Copyright 1951 by Langston Hughes. Copyright renewed 1979 by George Houston Bass.

Selections from *What do You Care What Other People Think?* by Richard P. Feynman. Reprinted by permission of W.W. Norton & Co.

C O N T E N T S

INTRODUCTION ix

1. The Orientation Class 1

2. Money Makes Cares
   A Tale from China 5

3a. The Tortoise and the Rabbit
    A Fable by Aesop 9

3b. The Tortoise and the Antelope
    A Tale of the Ngini People 11

4. The Koran 13

5. The Royal Commentary of the Inca
   by Inca Garcilaso de la Vega 15

6. Two Portraits
   by Rembrandt 18

7. The Parable of the Greedy Sons
   A Tale from Persia 19

8. A Man Who Couldn't See and A Man Who Couldn't Walk
   A Tale of the Hopi Indians 21

9. An Unlucky Man?
  A Tale from Nigeria 25

10. Life and Death
  A Tale of the Blackfoot Indians 27

11. The Symposium
  by Plato 29

12. Truth and Falsehood
  A Middle Eastern Folk Tale 31

13. A Speech to the National American
  Woman Suffrage Association 1890
  by Elizabeth Cady Stanton 33

14. The Tower of Babel
  The Bible 35

15. Maxims
  by La Rochefoucauld 37

16. The Knight's Tale
  by Geoffrey Chaucer 39

17. The Republic
  by Plato 41

18. The Life of Lycurgus
  by Plutarch 43

19a. Letters
  by Paul Cezanne 47

19b. Mont Sainte-Victoire
  by Paul Cezanne 49

20. A Case Study in Medical Ethics 51

21. Frankenstein
    by Mary Shelley 53

22. The Narrative of the Life of Fredrick Douglass
    by Fredrick Douglass 57

23. The Peloponnesian Wars
    by Thucydides. 59

24. Buddy
    by Langston Hughes. 61

25. The Souls of Black Folk
    by W.E.B. du Bois. 63

26. Pensées
    by B. Pascal 65

27. The Making of a Scientist
    by Richard Feynman 67

28. The Theaetetus
    by Plato. 71

29. A Lesson for Kings
    A Tale from India. 73

30. The Ethics
    by Aristotle 75

INTRODUCTION

As the world changes, so must the ways we teach and learn. Our world is becoming more interconnected, bringing together people with diverse backgrounds and differing perspectives. Technology places volumes of information at our fingertips. Such skills as problem-solving in groups, processing and evaluating new information, and working with diverse groups of people are more critical than ever to students' success. Students must now also learn how to teach themselves.

The Touchstones Discussion Project offers students and teachers the tools to meet the demands of this emerging environment. Students of all backgrounds and skill levels, across the United States and around the world, currently participate in Touchstones. In their weekly Touchstones Discussion classes, students learn strategies to help them navigate their way through school and through life. Touchstones helps students learn to process information, ask the right questions, and enlist the help of others in making decisions. As they listen, explore, co-operate, and solve problems, they become true collaborators in their own learning. They learn that life is not always about answers being right or wrong, but rather about decisions being better or worse.

Not only do students learn how to learn, teachers learn a new way to teach. The Touchstones Method offers teachers a powerful, new approach to group discussion that results in fully active and eager participation by the students. Eventually, the students themselves take the lead in the process. By bridging the gap between students' schoolwork and their experiences outside of school, Touchstones Discussions bring the classroom to life.

Skills

Touchstones Discussions develop skills that students will use in all of their classes, and they help students adopt a more responsible attitude toward their entire education. Examples of these skills and attitudes are

- Cooperating with their classmates, regardless of background,
- Stating ideas clearly,
- Respecting others' opinions,
- Identifying key issues of topics and texts,
- Asking questions to clarify discussion and improve understanding,
- Integrating text with experience and prior knowledge,
- Formulating complex ideas,
- Supporting opinions with evidence,
- Using questioning strategies,
- Exploring various interpretations of a text, and
- Confronting difficult problems that do not have clear right and wrong answers.

Touchstones Classes and the Texts

Typically, a class in the Touchstones Discussion Project has the following parts and shape:

- Students do not prepare before class.
- The whole class, including the teacher, sits in a circle.
- The teacher reads the text aloud as students follow along silently.
- Students do individual work.
- Students do small group work.
- The teacher asks an open-ended question to start discussion.
- Students do not raise their hands.
- Ground rules are followed.

The thirty texts in this volume are collected from male and female authors from a wide range of cultures throughout history. This variety allows and encourages students to experiment with different perspectives and alternative points of view, and allows them to apply the textual material to their own lives. Students begin to ask not only "What does the author really mean by this passage?" but also "How does this text apply to my life?"

The Role of the Teacher

The teacher's role in working with the Touchstones program is noticeably different from the teacher's role in other classes, especially in relation to the whole class discussions. The main point for teachers to keep in mind is that, in these Touchstones classes, they are not imparting information or knowledge but instead are cultivating skills and promoting changes in the attitudes of their students. This means that teachers should resist the temptation to give background information about authors or cultures and should not praise or correct students with respect to their opinions about the texts. Rather, the proper role is to try to generate those conditions, suggested by the exercises for each of the classes outlined in the *Teacher's Guide*, that enhance cooperation among students, help produce fertile uses for the texts, and help students view serious texts as "friendly." Nevertheless, teachers are still teachers with responsibilities, and discipline problems should be dealt with in whatever manner is usual and effective.

Organization of the Room

Touchstones classes never take place in a room with chairs or desks arranged in the familiar rows, where most students only see the back of the head of the student in front of them. Instead, chairs usually need to be moved at least three times in the course of the period: first, to form a single circle; second, to form groups of three to five; and third, to reform a large circle. Cooperation can occur only when you are facing the people you are trying to cooperate with, whether that is three, four, or twenty-nine other students. Reasonably accurate circles also make it harder for pairs of students to have side conversations while another student is explaining what he or she believes. Side conversations are a mark of disrespect, and they inhibit the mutual respect Touchstones Discussions try to foster. Touchstones classes use many such devices to instill the mutual and self-respect that lead to cooperation. And respect and cooperation are major steps toward taking responsibility for teaching others and oneself.

Teacher's Guides

The *Teacher's Guide* for this volume contains information to help teachers make the most of Touchstones Discussions. For each lesson, there is an orientation section detailing that class. These will include the following:

- Purpose statement for the lesson,
- Introduction to the lesson,
- Summary of the text,
- Possible question for discussion,
- Detailed lesson plan, and
- Student worksheets for individual and small group work.

The *Teacher's Guides* also include a variety of tools to help teachers throughout the year, including benchmarks and evaluation sheets that help teachers plan for each lesson and evaluate the group's strengths and weaknesses.

Additional support is available through Touchstones teacher workshops, the Touchstones website at www.touchstones.org, or by calling our office at 800-456-6542.

The Orientation Class

You, your classmates, and your teacher are about to begin a class which differs in some ways from your regular classes. The purpose of this class is to enable you to gain certain skills that will help you profit more from your regular classes. The new class is a discussion class. You will be talking to one another as well as to your teacher. We are all familiar with discussions because we have all discussed problems, feelings, opinions, and experiences with friends and relatives all of our lives. However, the discussions you will have in this class differ in some ways from your previous experiences.

Unlike your regular classes, in Touchstones discussion classes,

    a. everyone sits in a circle,

    b. the teacher is a member of the group and will help, but isn't an authority with the correct answers,

    c. there is no hand raising, instead everyone will learn how to run the discussion, and

    d. there is no preparation.

Unlike discussions which happen outside of class with friends and relatives, in Touchstones classes,

  a. discussions involve everyone in the class, your friends as well as students you don't know very well,

  b. discussions are about readings from the Touchstones book and not just your own concerns and experiences, and

  c. discussions occur once a week at a scheduled time, begin with a question asked by the teacher, and end when the teacher decides or when the bell rings.

Because of these differences, everyone must follow certain ground rules.

GROUND RULES

1. **Read the Text Carefully.** In Touchstones discussions your opinions are important, but these opinions are your thoughts about the text.

2. **Listen to What Others Say and Don't Interrupt.** A discussion cannot occur if you don't listen carefully to what people say.

3. **Speak Clearly.** For others to respond to your opinions, everyone must be able to hear and understand you.

4. **Give Others Your Respect.** A discussion is a cooperative exchange of ideas and not an argument or a debate. You may become excited and wish to share your ideas, but don't talk privately to your neighbor. In a Touchstones class, you will talk publicly for the whole class.

GOALS: WHAT YOU CAN GAIN FROM TOUCHSTONES DISCUSSION CLASSES

You will learn to

    a. listen better to what others say,

    b. explain your own ideas,

    c. speak and work with others whether you know them or not,

    d. receive correction and criticism from others,

    e. ask about what you don't understand,

    f. admit when you're wrong,

    g. think about questions for which the answers are uncertain,

    h. learn from others,

    i. teach others,

    j. teach yourself, and

    k. become more aware of how others see you.

2
Money Makes Cares
A Tale from China

Chen was a rich man who lived many years ago. He had so much money that he was always busy investing it, lending it, and paying taxes. From morning to night he never had a moment's peace. He had little time to eat—he never had dinner until late at night.

His wife pitied him for all the worries he had, and kept saying to him, "Look after yourself. Please don't work yourself to death." Chen agreed with her, but he did not know how to stop working.

His neighbor, Ti, was very poor. He and his wife together earned just enough to keep themselves alive. Ti was a good workman, and it was usually evening before he stopped work. Then he went home, gave his wife the money he had earned, and worried about nothing else. If he was in a good mood, he sang songs. That was his only amusement; at least it didn't cost any money.

The sounds of Ti singing and of Ti and his wife talking could be heard in Chen's house. But Chen was too busy going through his checks and bills to pay attention. His wife, however, was saddened by the happy sounds.

When Chen finally sat down for his evening meal, the sounds from Ti's house could still be heard. Chen's wife said to him, "Listen, Ti sounds so happy, although he is so poor. We are so rich, and yet we are never happy."

"Have you never heard the proverb, 'The penniless man has plenty of time'?" asked Chen. "He can be happy because he is poor. It would be quite easy to make him quit singing. We need only give him some money." "If you do that, he will become even happier." answered his wife. "Wait a little while," said Chen. "If you still hear him singing, I will admit I was wrong."

Next morning Chen invited Ti to his house and gave him a great deal of money. Never having dreamed of such a gift, Ti could only stammer out, "Many thanks for your kindness." He took the money and rushed home excited to tell his wife all that had happened. Now he no longer went to work. He did nothing but wonder how to use the money. He couldn't decide. Now when he came home, he was late for dinner and gulped it down quickly. Naturally, he had no time for singing or playing. He couldn't sleep at night thinking about the money.

Chen and his wife listened carefully to hear what their neighbor Ti did. There was no sound of singing. "Was I right?" Chen asked his wife. His wife smiled and admitted he was right.

For two nights Ti could get no sleep. On the morning of the third day the God of Luck appeared before him and said, "Money makes cares. Think of that, and bother no more about it."

Ti understood and, leaping out of bed, he hurried and gave the money back to Chen.

Ti felt as though a weight had been taken off his heart. He went home and slept like a baby. The next day he went out to work and, in the evening, the sound of singing and playing was once again heard coming from Ti's house.

3a The Tortoise and the Rabbit
A Fable by Aesop

One day a rabbit watched a tortoise walking slowly. He began to make fun of the tortoise's short legs and very, very slow pace. The tortoise laughed and said, "Rabbit, though you can run like the wind, I will beat you in a race." The rabbit couldn't believe what he heard. He thought it was impossible and accepted the challenge.

They asked a fox to set up a racecourse. On the day agreed upon, they met at the starting line. The two started together. However, once the rabbit was far ahead, he stopped at the side of the road. Trusting his natural speed, he relaxed and fell asleep. The tortoise all this while never stopped for a moment. He walked on with a slow and steady pace to the end of the racecourse. Finally, the rabbit woke up and ran on as fast as he could. When he reached the finish line, he saw the tortoise already there resting after the exhausting race.

The Tortoise and the Antelope
A Tale of the Ngini People

An antelope and a tortoise once had an argument. The antelope said, "Tortoise, are you able to run with me?" And the tortoise replied, "Of course I can." "Then tomorrow," said the antelope, "we'll race in the fields from the large tree near the hill to the stream." The tortoise was surprised at what he had agreed to do. He immediately went to tell the other tortoises what had happened. "The antelope and I were talking about running and somehow I agreed to race him tomorrow. My friends, you must come along and help me." The tortoises went to the field, and the tortoise who had to race placed them in a line, from the large tree to the stream. They were all hidden in the tall grass when the antelope arrived. The antelope saw his opponent by the tree, and said, "Come on, Tortoise, let's run." Then the antelope set off as hard and fast as he could. He ran and ran, and finally called out, "Tortoise, how are you doing?" From way up ahead of him, he heard a tortoise reply, "I've passed there long ago." So the antelope ran even harder. Finally, he called out again, "Tortoise where are you now?" Again from far out in front he heard a tortoise. "I'm up here. I passed there long ago." The antelope had been running hard and was exhausted. When he heard this second reply, the antelope gave up and left the field.

The 4 Koran

II, 178

O you believers! Revenge is allowed if someone is murdered: a man for a man, a slave for a slave, a woman for a woman. But for the criminal who is forgiven to some degree by the injured person, prosecute him according to the law and be merciful. This reduction of the punishment is a mercy from God. Whoever goes against it will have a painful death.

V, 45

And God says the following: A life for a life, an eye for an eye, a nose for a nose, an ear for an ear, a tooth for a tooth, and so on for other wounds. But whoever, out of kindness, does not ask for vengeance will be blessed. Whoever judges against what God says is a wrongdoer.

IV, 17

Forgiveness is given by God to those who do evil in ignorance and then are quickly sorry for what they have done. They are the ones God forgives.

IV, 18

Forgiveness is not for those who do nothing good until they are about to die, nor for those who die without believing in God. For all these people the end will be painful.

5

The Royal Commentary of the Inca
by Inca Garcilaso de la Vega

Pedro Serrano's ship sank near an island. He was a strong swimmer, and he alone of the crew reached it. However, as he got out of the water exhausted but alive, he saw he had reached a desert. There were neither people nor water, neither trees nor even grass. The first night he was desperate and depressed. He wished he had drowned. That way, at least, he would have died quickly. However, when morning came, he found some crabs nearby. This gave him hope and he ate them raw. Days later, large turtles came ashore. He caught one, turned it on its back, and killed it with the knife he still had. He ate the meat and was forced to drink the blood because he had no water. He used the empty shells of these turtles to catch the rainwater. Much painful experience taught him which turtles were too large and which he could catch. He accumulated many turtle shells and stocked supplies of food and water. It then seemed that if he could get fire, he would have all he needed—cooked food and smoke to signal passing ships.

His desert island had no stones, only sand. So he swam into the sea and dived to the bottom for stones. Back on land, he took the best, broke them against one another, and then rubbed one against his knife. Finally, he struck a few sparks. He tore his shirt up and was finally able to start a fire. He took dried seaweed to keep it going, but he had to spend all his time to protect it from the rain. So he built a hut from turtle shells to protect the fire and keep it going. But even then he could never leave it unattended for very long. With constant effort and struggle, he lived this way for three years. When ships passed, he always sent up his smoke signals, but none ever stopped. Once again, he became very depressed and wished to die.

Constant exposure to the weather had grown so much hair on his body that he looked more like an animal than a man. One afternoon to his great surprise he saw the tracks of another man on his island. The man had come ashore on a plank from a sinking ship. When they came face to face, both were startled. Each thought the other was a demon and ran away, praying to God. However, when they heard each other's prayers, they realized they had been wrong. They ran toward one another, embraced, and cried about their good fortune and misfortune.

They soon divided the tasks. When Pedro looked for food, the other cared for the fire. In a few days, however, they quarreled, almost fought and separated. One accused the other of not taking care of things as he should, though it was never clear whether this was true or merely what was felt. Soon after, they realized how foolish they had been and felt grateful neither had killed the other. They asked one another's forgiveness, became friends, and began over again. Many times they both wished nothing more than to lie down and die and end their torment. However, they remained alive, waiting. In the seventh year, a boat finally approached the island. They ran out into the water shouting prayers and passages from the Bible so the sailors would realize they were men and not animals or demons. Many writers have made up stories of shipwrecked sailors in lonely places, but Pedro Serrano lived what these writers only imagined. Because of his courage in staying alive, the island now bears his name.

Two Portraits
by Rembrandt

(Please see page 77 for the artwork.)

7
The Parable of the Greedy Sons
A Tale from Persia

There was once a hardworking and generous farmer who had several lazy and greedy sons. On his deathbed he told them that they would find his treasure by digging in a certain field. As soon as the old man was dead, the sons hurried to the field and dug it up from one end to the other.

They found no gold at all. Believing that their generous father had probably given the gold away, they abandoned the search. Finally, they decided that since they had already dug up the land, they might as well plant a crop. They planted wheat, had a good harvest, sold it, and made a big profit.

After they harvested the wheat, they wondered again whether the gold might still be there. So they dug the field again. Once again, they found no gold, but they planted more wheat with the same result.

After several years of this they stopped being lazy, got used to hard work, and became honest and happy farmers. They also became wealthy through their hard work and stopped thinking about the treasure. Finally they understood their father's trick as his way of teaching them.

The teacher, like the farmer, is also faced with students who are impatient, confused, and greedy like the farmer's sons. He has to get them to do something which he knows is good for them, but whose true purpose is hidden from them because they are so young.

8
A Man Who Couldn't See
and A Man Who Couldn't Walk
A Tale of the Hopi Indians

A long time ago there was an earthquake at the village of Oraibi. Fearing their village would be destroyed, all the villagers fled Oraibi leaving behind two men who weren't able to escape. These were a blind man and a man who couldn't walk. Frightened, the blind man called to the other man to ask what happened.

"The earth trembled," he responded, "and everyone has left. Come to my house."

"I can't," said the blind man. "You come here."

"I can't walk," responded the man who had not walked from birth. "But I can see. Take your stick and I'll tell you how to walk here."

So the blind man took his stick and walked slowly in the direction his friend told him.

"That worked very well," said the blind man. "Why don't we try to get away from here? I'll carry you on my back and you tell me the way."

So the man who couldn't walk got onto the back of the man who couldn't see. He turned the blind man's head in the direction they needed to go.

A short distance from the village a large animal passed in front of them.

"What is that?" asked the man who could see. "It is large and nearly black but not quite black."

The blind man had been a great hunter in his youth. He asked for more details and then realized what it was.

"It's an elk," he said. "Take out the bow and arrows." His friend handed over the bow and arrow and told the blind man where to aim. At the proper moment he said, "Shoot now!" The blind man released the arrow and they killed the elk. Now they wanted to cut the elk for meat.

"Put my hand near the elk," said the blind man. "With an arrow I can remove some meat."

They worked hard, the one giving directions, the other using the arrow to remove some meat. Then together they made a fire. While the elk roasted, the juices exploded. They were both startled and jumped up. The man who couldn't walk suddenly was cured and the blind man found he could see again. They were very excited throughout the day. At night, however, they were afraid to go to sleep because they thought they might return to what they were.

"If I close my eyes," said the blind man, "I might not be able to open them again."

"If I stop moving and sleep," said his companion, "I might never walk again. Let's keep one another up."

So each made sure the other stayed awake. In the morning the sun rose. The blind man saw the dawn. His friend stood up and stretched. They followed the tracks of the villagers and finally found them hiding in the north. The villagers were surprised to see them, having given up hope for these two.

"You were blind and lame. How did you both survive?"

"We survived together," they said, "and now we can both see and walk. And we can all return to our village which is still standing."

So the two led the villagers back to their homes. If these two had not brought the people back, the villagers would never have seen their homes again.

9
An Unlucky Man?
A Tale from Nigeria

There was once a poor man who had nothing but scraps for himself and his wife to eat. Nearby lived a rich man with many farms, children, and animals. One day, a man far richer than either the poor man or the rich man passed by on the road. However, the traveler wore rags, and he looked like a beggar. He approached the rich farmer and greeted him. But the rich farmer said, "How dare you speak to me? For all I know, you have some dreadful disease." So the traveler went on, and came to the poor man's farm. "Hello, how are you?" he said. As soon as the poor farmer heard the traveler, he asked his wife to take their scraps and prepare food for their visitor. The traveler in rags took the food, ate it, and thanked his host.

When the traveler reached home, he said, "I must reward the man who was kind to me." He filled a box with money. Then he took his daughter back to the area near the farms. "Do you see that man working there with his wife?" he asked. His daughter saw them. "Take this box and give it to him." The daughter obeyed, and approached the poor man. "I was told to bring this to you," she said. The poor man stared at it but didn't look inside. "Please, first take it to my rich neighbor. Let him take as much as he wants and leave us the rest." The girl obeyed him and approached the other farmer. The rich farmer opened the box and saw the money. He filled his pockets with all of the money and had his servants put flour into the container. "I've taken some. You can return the rest to my neighbor," he said to the girl. When the poor man received the box again and saw there was some flour in it, he was delighted. "Thanks to God," he said. "Pour it into this pot." The girl did as she was told and departed.

Her father, the very rich traveler, had been watching everything from a distance. As he realized what was happening, he became more and more enraged. "If you put an unlucky man into a jar of oil, he would emerge quite dry. I wanted that poor man to have some luck, but he was made to be unlucky, and nothing will change him."

10

Life and Death
A Tale of the Blackfoot Indians

Once there were only two people in the world, a man and a woman. They met as they traveled around and the woman said, "You and I should come to an agreement and then decide how future people will live." "I agree," said the man, "but only provided I have the first say in everything." The woman accepted as long as she could have the last word.

The man began thinking about how the new people should look. "Our children and grandchildren should have eyes and mouths in their faces. I think it would be best if these were straight up and down. The mouth should begin at the chin and end at the forehead." "I agree," said the woman, "that they should each have two eyes and a mouth, but they should start on one side of the face and go across to the other." "Very well," said the man. "How will these people work? Their hands need fingers, many fingers. Ten on each hand would be good." "Oh no," said the woman. "That would far too many. With so many, the fingers will get in one another's way. There shall be four fingers and one thumb on each hand."

They went on in this way until they had decided everything about their descendants. Then the woman asked what they should do about life and death: should people live forever or should they die? This was very hard for them to agree on. Finally the man made a suggestion. "I'll throw this stick into the water. If it floats, people will live forever. If it sinks, they will die." He threw the stick into the water and it floated. "No," said the woman, "we mustn't decide that way. I'll throw in this rock. If the rock floats, people will live forever. If it sinks, they will die." The woman threw in the rock and it sank. "There," she said. "It's better for people to die. If they didn't die, they would never feel sorry for one another. There would be neither sympathy nor pity in the world. And people would never help one another." When the man heard what she said, he agreed with her. "Yes, let it stay that way."

Sometime later the woman had a daughter. After a short time, the daughter became sick and died. The woman became very sad that people did not live forever. So she said to the man, "I was wrong. Let's talk about life and death again and reconsider." The man listened and thought about it. Finally he said, "No, we have settled it once and for all."

The Symposium
by Plato

Socrates and Diotima had been discussing love. Diotima disagreed with Socrates' account. She stopped him and said, "Socrates, you don't describe love very well. That's because you're thinking about what it's like to be loved. Instead you should focus on what it's like to love. Let me tell you a story that will help.

"Aphrodite is the goddess of Beauty, and is herself the most beautiful of all the goddesses. On the day she was born, there was a great party. One of the guests was Resource. He, as his name suggests, is very resourceful and inventive. He is the son of Skill. After dinner the goddess Need came to the door begging. She had heard the noise from the party and wanted to satisfy her unsatisfiable needs. Now, at just this moment, Resource wandered out into the garden. He had had too much to drink and fell into a heavy sleep. Need saw this as her great opportunity. If she could have a child with Resource, she thought it would help lessen her poverty. So she slept with Resource. Their child was Love.

"Because Love was conceived on the day Aphrodite was born, he became her follower. He is attracted to all beautiful things and people. As the son of Resource and Need he is similar to both parents. He always needs something. He is not delicate and lovely as most of us picture him. Rather, he is harsh and dry, barefoot and homeless. He always feels his mother's poverty. But he is also like his father. He uses all his father's resourcefulness and invention as he pursues beauty. He is brave, energetic, a great hunter, very impetuous, and full of tricks and plans. He is at once full of wisdom and also full of desire. He is neither like humans who die nor like gods who never die. On the same day, he can be both. When all goes well, he is alive and blooming. But later he might start dying, and then be born again through the resourcefulness he inherited from his father. Like his mother, he keeps needing more. Since love is a great seeker after truth, he wants what is truly beautiful. He keeps looking. But, if love finds out that what he loves is not really beautiful, he dies."

"I'm sure what you say is right." said Socrates. "But what good can Love be to us humans?"

"Love includes every kind of longing for happiness and beauty," Diotima answered. "Everything we do is prompted by some kind of love. We don't realize clearly that those who we say love money or power or sport or music or knowledge are as truly lovers as those who love another person. In one sense they are all the same, though they disagree on what is truly beautiful."

12
Truth and Falsehood
A Middle Eastern Folk Tale

Once upon a time, Truth met Falsehood at a crossroads. Falsehood asked Truth how he was and whether he felt well. Truth answered, "It gets worse all the time." Truth looked miserable. He was very thin and dressed in rags. "I haven't eaten for a while," he said "and everywhere I go I find that more and more people dislike me. There are always fewer and fewer people who really love me and those are treated badly by others." "I'll show you how to be liked by people," answered Falsehood. "Just come with me. You'll dress well, eat well, and be happy. But you must do just as I do and never disagree with me in public— never disobey me or say I'm wrong."

Truth was so unhappy and hungry and cold that he agreed to do as Falsehood said. So they set off together. When they reached the nearest large city, they went to the first restaurant. Falsehood ordered a magnificent meal for both of them. They ate their fill, and stayed at the table a long, long time, until nearly everyone else had left the room. Then Falsehood clapped his hands and called the head-waiter. Because Falsehood was dressed so well, the head-waiter bowed low, and asked how he could serve or help them.

"I gave the boy who served us a hundred dollar bill an hour ago. How much longer must I wait for him to bring change?" asked Falsehood. The boy was called, and he said no one had given him a hundred dollar bill. Falsehood started to shout and appeared very angry. "This seemed such a fine restaurant," he said, "I would never have thought I would be cheated. It just shows that you can never tell anything at all by appearances. But I shall tell all my friends never to come here again." With that, he threw a hundred dollar bill on the table, and told the head-waiter to bring him the change.

Because he was afraid this fine gentlemen would give the restaurant a bad name, the head-waiter did not pick up the money from the table. Instead, he gave Falsehood the change he demanded. Falsehood stormed out of the restaurant and Truth followed. When they were safely outside, Falsehood burst out laughing and said, "There! That's how I make things work out for me." But Truth said, "I would rather die of hunger than do what you do."

13

A Speech to the National American Woman Suffrage Association 1890
by Elizabeth Cady Stanton

Some men tell us we must be patient and persuasive; that we must be womanly. My friends, what is man's idea of womanliness? It is for us to have a manner which pleases him—quiet, deferential, submissive, approaching him as a servant does a master. He wants no self-assertion on our part, no defiance, no vehement accusation of him as a robber and a criminal ... while the darkest page of human history contains the crimes against women—shall men still tell us to be patient, persuasive, womanly?

What do we know yet of being womanly? The women we have been so far, with few exceptions, are only echoes of men. Man has spoken in the powerful places in the State, the Church and the Home. Man has made the laws, the beliefs and the customs which govern every relation in life, and women have simply echoed all his thoughts and walked in the paths he set out. And this is being womanly! When Joan of Arc led the French army to victory against the English, I dare say the English knights thought her unwomanly. When Florence Nightingale, in search of blankets to comfort the soldiers in the Crimean War, cut through all the men's orders and red tape, and commanded with strength and determination those who guarded the supplies to "unlock the doors and not talk to her about proper authorities when brave men were shivering in their beds," no doubt she was called unwomanly... I consider she took the most womanly way of accomplishing her object. Patience and persuasiveness are virtues when talking to children and feebleminded adults, but to those who have the gift of reason and understand the principles of justice, it is our duty to speak and act up to the highest light that is in them... .

14
The Tower of Babel
The Bible

Once upon a time, all the world spoke a single language and used the same words. As men journeyed in the east, they came upon a plain in the land of Shinar and settled there. "Come," they said, "let us build ourselves a city and a tower with its top in the heavens and make a name for ourselves; or we shall be separated and spread out all over the earth." Then the Lord came down to see the city and tower which mortal men were building, and he said, "Here they are, one people with a single language, and now they have started to do this; from now on, nothing they have a mind to do will be beyond their reach. I will go down there and confuse their speech, so that they will not understand what they say to one another." So the Lord separated them from there all over the earth, and they left off building the city. The city was called Babel, because the Lord made a babble of the common language causing the people to scatter everywhere since they could no longer understand each other.

15

Maxims
by La Rochefoucauld

1. Why do we tell our deepest secrets to others? Usually because we want them to feel sorry for us or admire us.

2. It is very difficult to love someone we don't respect. But it is just as difficult to love someone we respect much more than we respect ourselves.

3. Everyone dresses up and acts the way he wants others to think of him. So you might say that the whole world is made up of people playing different parts.

4. Some people always say and do foolish things. They are valuable because they serve a useful purpose. They would upset everything if they changed their behavior.

5. Lucky people do not try to improve themselves very much. Usually good luck makes their stupid or bad actions work out successfully. This

makes them imagine it's really because they were right or good or smart.

6. If we ourselves had no faults, we wouldn't get so much enjoyment from seeing the faults of other people.

The Knight's Tale
by Geoffrey Chaucer

Prince Arcite and Prince Palamon, both from Thebes, were the closest of friends. They were captured in war and locked up together in a prison tower in Athens. One day Palamon looked into a courtyard and saw Emily, a beautiful princess. He immediately fell in love with her. His friend Arcite, hearing Palamon speaking about her aloud, came to the window. He too immediately fell in love with the same woman. The men quarreled. They became jealous of one another, and their friendship was destroyed. Sometime later Arcite was freed from prison on the condition that if he were ever found in or near Athens, he would be killed.

When Arcite heard about his freedom, he felt sick. He cried and cursed the day of his birth. "My freedom is worse than my prison. Here in this tower, I would have been happy forever. Palamon, you are lucky. You, at least, can look out of the window and see Emily everyday. And fortune can change. Though you are in prison, you are near her. You may be released and have the woman you desire. But I must leave and live at home in Thebes, an exile from where I wish to be. We never know what we want and pray for. We always look for happiness in the wrong place. I was convinced that if I could only get out of prison my happiness would be a certainty. Now I am free, but since I cannot see Emily, I am like a corpse. In searching for happiness, we are like a drunk who knows well enough that he has a home, but doesn't know where it is.

Palamon, when he learned the news, screamed in anger. "Arcite, you've won. You can walk freely in Thebes, your home. You can raise an army and go to war with Athens. Perhaps through some bold attack or a treaty, you will gain Emily for your wife. Your position is so much better than mine. You are a prince again and free. I must remain here dying in a cage. Fate which rules the world, is cruel. It treats men no differently from animals. But an animal may, at least, do what it pleases. Men, however, are often jailed for no reason at all and others who do harm go free. There is great misery in the world."

So the summer passed and its long nights increased the torments of the princes. I don't know which of them had it worse. Palamon was condemned to perpetual imprisonment until he dies. Arcite, exiled from Athens on pain of death, could never see his beloved again. Let me put the question to you, lovers and readers. Who had the worst of it? One of them can see Emily every day from his window, but stays in prison forever. The other, free to go where he pleases, may never see Emily again.

17
The Republic
by Plato

Are people good because they want to be? Or are they good because they are afraid to be bad? To answer these questions let us pretend we can give both the good and the bad person the freedom and power to do whatever they please. Then in our imaginations we can see what they will do. I think the good person will be no different from the bad person, for he is really as selfish as the bad man. Only fear of the law makes him good. Let me tell you a story about a man who had such freedom.

People say that this man was a shepherd in the service of the king of Lydia. After a great rainstorm and an earthquake, the ground opened up where he was caring for sheep, and he went into the opening in the earth. The story goes on to say that he saw many wonderful things there, among which was a large bronze model of a horse with little doors on the side. When he looked in, he saw the body of a giant with a gold ring on its finger. He took the ring and left.

When the shepherds held their monthly meeting to report to the king about his flocks, he also attended, wearing the ring. While he was sitting there twisting the ring on his finger, he happened to turn it so that the stone faced his palm. When he did this, the story goes on, he became invisible. Those who sat around him could no longer see him. They spoke about him as if he were not there. He was amazed and twisted his ring once more. When he turned the stone out, he became visible again. He tested this many times, and found that the ring really possessed this power of making him invisible when he wanted. So with the help of this ring, he committed many crimes and took over the kingdom.

Now suppose we have two such rings. Let's give one to a good person and the other to an evil person. It is hard to believe that even a good man would stop himself from stealing and doing all kinds of other bad things, if he knew he would never get caught.

18

The Life of Lycurgus
by Plutarch

The city of Sparta in Greece was in confusion. Lycurgus was asked by the citizens to help them. Like a doctor who has a very sick patient, he realized that small changes and a few new laws would not help. He decided to change everything—both the laws and the way people lived their lives.

Because some were very rich and others very poor, he seized all the land, divided it up into equal pieces, and gave each citizen the same amount. Because people often desire great wealth, he stopped the use of gold and other precious metals as money. Instead, large chunks of iron which were worth very little were used as money. This stopped many evils such as robbery and bribery. But the cleverest and best law of this great lawgiver forced all the citizens to eat together. Lycurgus made all the citizens eat the same breads, meats, and other foods. This one law was the strongest blow against the desire for riches. The rich, who were forced always to eat with the poor, could not enjoy their wealth by using it or looking at it.

Lycurgus never put his laws into writing. He thought a greater security would result from the habits of action formed by the best lawgiver—education. He thought the education of children was the most important work of a lawgiver. Since he believed that children belonged primarily to the state rather than to their parents, he also regulated marriages and births. It was absurd, he thought, that people bred the best dogs and horses or cattle together but did not control the birth of children. He therefore planned it out that only the best men and women would have the most children. Since he believed that people who speak a great deal say little, children were taught to be silent and pack much meaning into few words. Here are a few examples. A man kept giving the Spartan King Leonides a lot of good advice, but at the wrong time and place. When the man finally paused, the king said, "Well said, elsewhere." A foreigner kept asking the Spartan, Demaratus, to name the best citizen of Sparta. At last Demaratus answered, "He that is least like you."

Lycurgus also kept unnecessary foreigners out of Sparta, and did not allow Spartans to travel abroad. Strange habits and customs, he believed, introduce new ideas, and he protected against this as most people protect against disease. Having finished his work, he called the citizens together. He wished, he said, to get the approval of the gods for his work at the temple at Delphi. However, he asked the Spartans to swear not to change the laws until he returned. When they all took the oath, he left. After visiting the shrine, he starved himself to death. Because Lycurgus never returned to Sparta, the citizens had to keep their oath. Lycurgus believed that a statesman should serve the state and be a good example even in death.

Letters
by Paul Cezanne

To Louis Aurenche:

In your letter you talk about what I have accomplished in my paintings. I accomplish more every day, although it's hard to do. This is because knowledge of artistic technique is necessary to express our feelings. This knowledge can be acquired only through long experience. Of course, the most important thing is to have a strong feeling for nature, and I certainly have that.

To Emile Bernard:

I progress very slowly, for nature reveals herself to me in very complex ways, and the work required to paint this is endless. You have to look at what you're painting, feel it very exactly, and express yourself distinctly and with force.

To Emile Bernard:

I must always come back to this. Painters must devote themselves entirely to the study of nature, and try to paint pictures which will educate people. Talking about art is almost useless for the painter.

Mont Sainte-Victoire
by Paul Cezanne

(Please see page 78 for the artwork.)

20

A Case Study in Medical Ethics

A five-year-old girl has a serious kidney disease. Her kidneys have stopped working. The doctors are confident that if she gets a new kidney she will get well. However, if she doesn't get a new kidney she will die. The doctors discuss this procedure with the parents who agree with plans to operate and give her a new kidney. A new kidney will be successfully implanted only if it comes from a very close relative. Tests are made on the mother, father and two younger brothers. The brothers are thought to be too young, and the mother turns out to be medically unsuitable. The father, however, is a close match, and the doctors are sure one of his kidneys can be transplanted successfully.

The father, however, after some thought, decides not to donate a kidney to his daughter. He admits to the doctors that he doesn't have the courage. He asks the doctor not to tell the family this, but to say that his kidney is not a good match. He is afraid of what his family will think if they are told the truth. The doctor doesn't want to lie to the family, but finally tells them that the man cannot donate a kidney for "medical reasons."

21
Frankenstein
by Mary Shelley

Years ago, Dr. Victor Frankenstein had watched his creature stir and breathe for the first time in his laboratory rooms. The doctor had recoiled in horror at how ugly the creature was and had run away from the creature as soon as he was brought to life. Over the years, the creature wandered and hid up in the mountains of the Swiss Alps. He had learned to speak by observing a family in a mountain valley. Now, the creature sat in a cave with Dr. Frankenstein, his Creator, talking with him for the first time. Human speech enabled him precisely to describe his situation and his feelings of sadness and loneliness to the doctor.

"From studying human society, I realized that important ancestors and wealth are honored by people most of all. A person might be respected with only one of these but without either, he is considered a slave. He is then doomed to work long hard days at little pay or none at all for those who control the wealth and power of a country. And yet I am worse off than the poorest of the poor! What am I? I knew nothing of my creator or how I was created. I have no money, no friends, no ancestors, no property. Furthermore, I am deformed and ugly. I am not even the same nature as man. I am more agile and quicker than they and can live on coarser food. I can stand heat and cold better, and am larger and stronger. Yet I am isolated. When I look around I see no one at all like me. What am I, then, a monster, a blot on the earth? When people see me, they run away. No one wants any contact with me.

"I can't describe the agony these thoughts cause me. I try to escape them and distract myself but my sorrow only increases as I learn more about people. Often I wish I had stayed alone in the deepest forest. I wish I had known or felt nothing beyond the mere sensations of hunger, thirst, and heat. Knowledge can be so strange. Once you learn something, it sticks with you, it clings to you. Sometimes I want to shake off all thought and feeling. But I have learned there is no way to cut off these feelings of mental pain. I admire goodness and nobility and all the other wonderful and beautiful things I notice in the people I have watched. But I am shut out from all contact with them. And this has turned my generous thoughts into feelings of anger. My only connection with humans has been without their knowing what I was, without their seeing me. But this only increases my desire to become one among other people. No father had watched over me as an infant, no mother had blessed me with smiles. Or if they had, I have no memory. My past life is a blank in which I can distinguish nothing.

I only remember being just as I am now. I have never seen anyone who resembles me. The question that comes to me again and again through my groans is: What am I?

22

The Narrative of the Life of Fredrick Douglass
by Fredrick Douglass

I got this idea of how I might learn to write when I was working in Durgin and Bailey's shipyard in Baltimore. There I often watched the ship's carpenters saw the wood and prepare it for use. They would write on the wood the name of the part of the ship where it would be used. When a piece of timber was intended for the left side, it would be marked "L." A piece for the front of the ship on the left side was marked "L.F." One for the aft of the ship—the part to the back—on the right was marked "R.A." By watching them I soon learned the names of these letters and what they meant when put on a piece of wood. I immediately started copying them and in a short time was able to write these four letters: L, R, F, A. This was my first step in learning to write.

I then had to find a way to learn still more letters. To accomplish this, I devised the following plan. Whenever I met any boy I knew could write, I would tell him I could write as well as he. Usually he would say, "I don't believe you. Let me see you try it." I would then make the letters I was lucky enough to learn and ask him to beat that. He would write down five or six letters or however many were needed. So by losing the bet, I would learn a few more letters. In this way I got a good many lessons in writing, which it is quite possible I should never have gotten in any other way. During this time, my only paper was a wooden fence or brick wall or pavement, and my pen and ink was a piece of chalk. With these, I learned how to write.

I then started copying the letters in a spelling book until I could make all of them without looking at the original letters. By this time, my little Master Thomas had gone to school and learned how to write. He had written his letters and words in a number of copy-books, which had then been brought home and laid aside. When I was in the house alone, I used to spend my time writing in the spaces left in these practice books. I wrote just what he had written. I continued doing this until my handwriting was very similar to that of Master Thomas. Thus after a long and tedious effort lasting years, I finally succeeded in learning how to write.

23

The Peloponnesian Wars
by Thucydides

The great cities of Athens and Sparta in Greece had been at war with one another for four years. At the end of the fourth year, some of the citizens of the city of Corcyra asked for assistance from the Athenians, while some of their fellow citizens, who were their enemies, asked the Spartans for help. So the war between the two cities entered the single city of Corcyra and became a civil war. In peace there would never have been the desire to invite outsiders in to help in local disputes. In peace and prosperity, states and individuals have better attitudes and feelings because they are not suddenly faced with terrible needs. But war takes away the easy supply of daily food and other goods. War proves a tough master, and brings people's characters down to the level of their needs. So at this point in the war each group in Corcyra called upon a foreign ally to help them against their enemies.

The conflict became so intense that even the normal meanings of words began to change. What in peacetime would be called a "reckless act" was now considered an act of courage. A thoughtful person was seen as a coward. An act of great violence showed that someone was a man. The person who proposed extreme actions was always trusted. A person who proposed compromise between the two sides was viewed with suspicion by everyone. Finally, even ties of blood and family became weaker than ties of loyalty to those of the same political party or gang. People in the same gang were willing to risk anything together. Their confidence in one another rested on having committed crimes together and planning more. Oaths of friendship and peace were now used merely to meet an immediate difficulty. They were broken as soon as one side felt strong enough. Men even became proud of this kind of dishonesty because it made them look smart.

There was no way out of all this once it began. Promises could no longer be believed. No oath could command respect. Everyone gave up hope for a permanent state of things and considered only their self-defense and self-interest. Life was now thrown into incredible confusion. Human nature always rebels against the law. But in Corcyra, desires were given complete freedom, revenge was placed above religion, and profit above justice. All this happened because of the devastating power of envy. And all men resorted to revenge. This set the example of doing away with laws which, though they might at one time protect one's enemies, might later protect oneself. This kind of conflict first emerged in Corcyra, and then spread to all the other cities of Greece as they were drawn into the war.

24 Buddy

by Langston Hughes

That kid's my buddy,
still and yet
I don't see him much.
He works downtown for twelve a week.
Has to give his mother Ten—
she says he can have
the other two
to pay his carfare, buy a suit,
coat, shoes,
anything he wants out of it.

25

The Souls of Black Folk
by W.E.B. du Bois

It is, then, the task of all honorable men of the twentieth century to see that in the future competition of races, the survival of the fittest shall mean the victory of goodness, beauty, and truth. We must preserve for future civilization all that is fine and noble and strong. We must not continue to reward greed, aggressiveness, and cruelty. To bring this hope to realization we are forced every day to turn more and more to a continuous study of the contacts between the races. This study must be honest and fair, and not colored by our wishes and fears.

In the civilized life of today, the contact of men and their relations to each other fall in a few main groups of forms of social communication. There is, first, the distance of homes to one another, the way in which neighborhoods group themselves, and which neighbors live next to which. Secondly, and in our times most importantly, there are economic relations—the methods by which individuals cooperate for earning a living, for the mutual satisfaction of needs, and for the production of wealth. Thirdly, there are political relations, the cooperation in social control, in group government, and in paying taxes. In the fourth place, there are the less obvious but very important forms of intellectual contact. These include the exchange of ideas through conversations, conferences, magazines, and libraries, and, especially, the formation within each community of public opinion. Connected with this are the various forms of social contact in every day life, in travel, theaters, houseparties, and weddings. Finally, there are the different forms of religious activity, moral teachings, and public service. These are the main ways in which human beings living in the same communities are brought in contact with each other.

Pensées
by B. Pascal

A man goes to the window to watch people passing by. If I happen to be passing by, can I say he went there to see me? No, for he is not thinking of me in particular. But what about a person who loves someone because she is beautiful. Does he love her? No, for a disease can destroy the beauty without destroying the person. Yet, this disease will put an end to his love for her.

And if someone loves me because I have a good memory or because I am very intelligent, do they love me? *Me*, myself? No, for I could lose these qualities and still be myself. But where is this "self," if it is neither in my body nor my soul? And anyway, how can you love a body or a soul except for the qualities it has? Could you love a soul all by itself? Of course not, and it would be wrong. Therefore, we don't love other people, but only their qualities.

27
The Making of a Scientist
by Richard Feynman

We used to go to the Catskill Mountains, a place where people from New York City would go in the summer. The fathers would all return to New York to work during the week and come back only for the weekend. On weekends, my father would take me for walks in the woods, and he'd tell me about interesting things that were going on in the woods. When the other mothers saw this, they thought it was wonderful and that the other fathers should take their sons for walks. They tried to work on them, but they didn't get anywhere at first. They wanted my father to take all the kids, but he didn't want to because he had a special relationship with me. So it ended up that the other fathers had to take their children for walks the next weekend.

The next Monday, when the fathers were all back at work, we kids were playing in a field. One kid said to me, "See that bird? What kind of bird is that?"

I said, "I haven't the slightest idea what kind of a bird it is."

He says, "It's a brown-throated thrush. Your father doesn't teach you anything!"

But it was the opposite. He had already taught me:

"See that bird?" my father had said, "It's a Spencer's warbler." (I knew he didn't know the real name.) "Well, in Italian, it's a *Chutto Lapottida*. In Portuguese, it's a *Bom da Pieda*. In Chinese, it's a *Chung-long-tah*, and in Japanese, it's a *Latano Tekeda*. You can know the name of that bird in all the languages of the world, but when you're finished, you'll know absolutely nothing whatever about the bird. You'll only know about humans in different places and what they call the bird. So let's look at the bird and see what it's *doing*—that's what counts." (I learned very early the difference between knowing the name of something and knowing something.)

He said, "For example, look: the bird pecks at its feathers all the time. See it walking around, pecking at its feathers?"

"Yeah."

He said, "Why do you think birds peck at their feathers?"

I said, "Well, maybe they mess up their feathers when they fly, so they're pecking them in order to straighten them out."

"All right," he said. "If that were the case, then they would peck a lot just after they've been flying. Then, after they're been on the ground a while, they wouldn't peck so much any more—you know what I mean?"

"Yeah."

He said, "Let's look and see if they peck more just after they land."

It wasn't hard to tell: There was not much difference between the birds that had been walking around a bit and those that had just landed. So I said, "I give up. Why does a bird peck at its feathers?"

"Because there are lice bothering it," he said. "The lice eat flakes of protein that come off its feathers." He continued, "Each louse has some waxy stuff on its legs, and little mites eat that. The mites don't digest it perfectly, so they emit from their rear ends a sugar-like material in which bacteria grow." Finally he said, "So you see, everywhere there's a source of food, there's *some* form of lice that finds it."

Now, I knew that it may not have been exactly a louse, that it might not be exactly true that the louse's legs have mites. That story was probably incorrect in *detail*, but what he was telling me was right in *principle*.

The Theaetetus
by Plato

There are many different ways to understand how we think and remember and how we make mistakes. When we explain how this happens to ourselves or others we often use more familiar images to help us imagine it. Here Socrates mentions two possibilities.

Socrates: Some people have suggested that our minds contain a material that is similar to a piece of wax. This material, like wax, can be larger or smaller. So different people can have different size pieces. Also in some people the wax-like material is harder than in others, or softer, or moister, or more or less pure. When we wish to remember anything which we have seen or heard or thought, we expose the waxy material to our thoughts or feelings. The material receives the imprint just as we might make an impression of some object in a piece of wax. And as long as this material holds the impression of our thoughts or feelings or what we have seen or heard, then we remember. But just like what happens in wax, the image can wear away. When that happens we say we have forgotten and no longer know. Some people are born with pure, deep, and abundant waxlike material. These people learn easily and don't get confused. Others have softer material. They learn easily but forget right away and make errors. Yet others have wax that is hard. These are difficult to teach but once they learn, they hold onto it for a long time. But we can also create other pictures and images to help us understand how our minds work.

We might say that our minds are similar to a bird cage. When we are born it is empty. Whenever we see or learn something, the colors or ideas come into us. They are like birds that enter into and stay in this cage. And when we experience different kinds of things, colors or sounds, these are like birds of different kinds that we take in. Now, some of these creatures are always flying around, some of these stay apart from others, some flock with others. So when we want to think about something or remember something we try to catch the right bird. If it's one that stays with others, we remember that too. Now sometimes it can be hard to get just the right bird, because some look similar to others and sometimes we think we will get one sort of bird and we either catch nothing or find we have the wrong one. In this case we say a person has made a mistake. So this is another way of thinking about how we think and what our minds are like. Which do you think is a better image of how we think? Or, are they both good but for different things?

29
A Lesson for Kings
A Tale from India

The king of Benares ruled his kingdom so justly and well that he had nothing left to do. So he decided to find out what failures and faults he himself had. He asked everyone in the city, but heard only how good he was. He thought this was because people were afraid of him. So in disguise, he went out into the countryside and asked the people about their king. But again he heard only praises of himself. So he decided to return to the city. As he and his charioteer traveled to his capital, they reached a very narrow trail with steep cliffs on both sides. Here they saw the king of Kosala and his charioteer. This king had also been out in his countryside trying to learn his own faults and failures. He, too, was returning because he heard nothing but praise. So the two chariots approached the narrow trail and the charioteers had to decide who should go first.

The chariot driver of the king of Benares spoke first, "My passenger is the king of Benares, so make way." But the other driver said, "My passenger is also a king." So the charioteer of the king of Benares thought about how to decide who should cross first. He thought he would ask how old each of the kings was, and the younger would make way for the older. But they were both the same age. Then he thought they should compare their power, and the most powerful would go first. But the kings were equal in power. Next he tried wealth, but here, too, they were the same. Next he asked about fame and family. But the two kings were equally famous and their families equally distinguished.

Finally he thought, "I will ask about the justice of this king of Kosala. The king who is less just will wait for the more just king to pass over." So he asked the charioteer, "In what way is your king just?" "The justice of the king of Kosala is this," said his charioteer. "The strong he overthrows by strength. The mild he subdues by mildness. He meets the good with goodness and the wicked with wickedness. That is what my king is like. What is your king's justice?"

The charioteer of the king of Benares answered, "The king of Benares conquers the evil by his goodness, the stingy with his gifts. He meets the speaker of lies with truth. That's what my king is like." After they had spoken, one of the charioteers and his king got out of their chariot and made way for the other king.

The Ethics
by Aristotle

Imagine that two people are friends. What if one of them changes; can they still remain friends? Suppose someone who was good and admirable becomes vicious and bad? Should we remain that person's friend or break it off? It seems difficult to remain friendly since we can't or mustn't feel affection for someone who is bad. If we do, we risk becoming bad ourselves since people tend to become like their friends. But should we break it off at once? We should do that only if we feel nothing can be done to change the person back to what they were. If someone can be set right, we should at least make the effort to rescue him. However, by breaking off the friendship, we do nothing wrong or absurd. We were not friendly with this sort of person. Since the friend has changed and we can't do anything about it to help and save him, we break off the friendship.

Now what if one person remains how he was, and the other becomes much better—more decent, or more excellent or such that they are no longer similar or equal? Can the one who improved remain friendly with the other who hasn't changed and grown? It doesn't seem possible. We can see this clearly where a wide separation develops. We often find that two people were friends in childhood. However, as they grow they become interested in very different things, and so they grow apart. They stop having any reason to talk or to do anything together. One might still like to do the things that a child would do while the other matures and grows. Can they still be friends? It's hard to see how. But should the one who has grown and changed treat the other as if they were never friendly? It doesn't seem right just to forget it entirely. One might continue to feel affection and concern for the other person, but not if the other person became bad and evil.

Lesson 19b, Mon

Lesson 6, Self-Portrait (1659)

Lesson 6, Portrait (1650)

Sainte-Victoire (1897)